WISDOM, INSIGHT, & INSTRUCTION

Wisdom, Insight, & Instruction

WII

QUINTARIUS GRIGSBY

Followers of the Way

While every precaution has been taken in the preparation of this book, the publisher assumes no responsibility for errors or omissions, or for damages resulting from the use of the information contained herein.

Wisdom, Insight, & Instruction: WII
First print, 2022.
ISBN: 978-0-578-38926-4
Written by Quintarius Grigsby.

Copyright © 2022 by Quintarius Grigsby

Scripture quotations are taken from the Holy Bible, King James Version®.

All rights reserved. This book contains material protected under International and Federal Copyright Laws and Treaties. Any unauthorized reprint or use of this material is prohibited. No part of this book may be reproduced or transmitted in any form or by any means, electronic or mechanical, including photocopying, recording, or by any information storage and retrieval system without express written permission of the publisher, except in the case of brief quotations embodied in critical reviews and certain noncommercial uses permitted by copyright law.

For bulk orders or other inquiries, email: services@fotheway.com.

CONTENTS

Introduction

~ 1 ~

The Importance of Spiritual Substance

4

~ 2 ~

Judgment on the Unruly Sheep

6

~ 3 ~

Be Humble and Fearless

8

~ 4 ~

Meat That Nourishes the Soul

11

~ 5 ~

God As Your Supplier

13

~ 6 ~

Understanding the War Within

16

~ 7 ~

Relationship Between A King and His Wife

18

~ 8 ~

The Power of A Will to Change

20

~ 9 ~

The Image of God Can Be Restored

23

~ 10 ~

Season for Planting

27

~ 11 ~

Impurities of Today's Knowledge

29

~ 12 ~

The War Between Wants and Needs

32

~ 13 ~

How To Discern Spiritual Energy and Defeat Gluttony

35

~ 14 ~

Obstacles Encountered During A Major Transition

38

~ 15 ~

When the Lord Transplants You in A New Environment

42

~ 16 ~

Standing in the Face of Adversity

45

~ 17 ~

Canceling Out Negativity

48

~ 18 ~

Only God Can Understand Good and Evil

50

CONCLUSION OF THE WHOLE MATTER - 53

ACKNOWLEDGMENTS

Foremost, I desire to acknowledge my Father, who is in heaven, my counselor, the source of my strength, and my Elohim (King and Judge). Since the beginning, the Most High has been with me, molding my character and directing my way. He has made me into a fine warrior and taught me the path of meditation and self-control. I pray that He shall forever be with me as I serve Him according to the Way of Truth. He has brought me forth out of the darkness as His very own Son (Sun). The One true living Elohim has caused me to be a shining light. Oh, how I love you and how I desire to forever follow in your footsteps. My soul shall make her boast in the Lord (Psalm 34:2).

I definitely have to acknowledge my wife and Queen, Chatassia, for being an excellent spouse and administrator. The Most High has truly anointed her with a fantastic gift, and without her, there are things I would not have accomplished in this current season of my life. She is the epitome of a good thing and the embodiment of the spirit of prudence. It is truly an honor and privilege to be your husband and life partner in advancing God's kingdom. I love you and pray you will continue growing into the woman and vessel the Most High designed you to be.

I thank you, Chatassia, for being my good thing in all sincerity and appreciation.

Introduction

In this book of wisdom and direction, I will cover the theme of *wisdom* and *knowledge* about specific experiences, goals, and challenges in life. Life can grant us some of the most tedious obstacles to help build our character and spiritual life. However, it is up to us to spend quality time with the Most High God and apply His instructions to develop a positive mindset relating to those experiences.

What are some of the circumstances you may be facing in this present moment? Hopefully, whatever your situation may be, the content within this book may help you along your quest for self-realization and overcoming. It's also essential for us, as believers, to pray for wisdom and insight. The most important gift the Most High God gives to us is wisdom if we're open to receiving.

According to the Oxford Dictionary, *wisdom* is the quality of having experience, knowledge, and good judgment. The quality of being wise is the soundness of an action or decision concerning the application of experience, knowledge, and good judgment. Wisdom brings forth direction and righteous judgment to apply to our daily lives. Proverbs 4:7 says, "Wisdom is the principal thing; therefore get wisdom: and with all thy getting, get understanding."[1]

Instructions are complementary to wisdom and insight. Instructions are detailed information expressing how something should be done, operated, or assembled. Instructions are provided by the Most High through His commandments. Proverbs 10:17 states, "He is in the way of life that keepeth instruction: but he that refuseth reproof erreth."

Insight is a part of the nature of the Spirit we should all strive to attain. It helps you have a deeper intuitive comprehension of all things. Insight is the capacity to gain an accurate and deep intuitive understanding of a person or thing. 2 Timothy 2:7 says, "Consider what I say, for the Lord will give you understanding in everything." Spending quality time with Christ will give you the understanding needed to pass every test of life you must face:

> *All Scripture is given by inspiration of God and is profitable for doctrine, reproof, correction, instruction in righteousness: That the man of God may be perfect, thoroughly furnished unto all good works*
> **-2 Timothy 3:16-17**

Throughout this book, I will share the wisdom the Most High has blessed me within its simplicity. I believe that lofty information introduced by others can sometimes cause confusion and make matters worse. Heavenly wisdom is from the Spirit of Truth; it does not overcomplicate things, even in times of great tribulation.

There is an essential need for encouragement through the Word of truth in this day and time. Truth opens our minds to the realms of spiritual enlightenment through the improvement of biblical scriptures. The Word brings forth the light of God's wisdom, and it has the power to restore our souls. Psalm 23:2-3 states, "He maketh me to lie down in green pastures: he leadeth me beside the still waters. He restoreth my soul: he leadeth me in the paths of righteousness for his name's sake." Without the Word, there is no deliverance, restoration, sanctification, or salvation.

> *Thy word is a lamp unto my feet, and a light unto my path.*
> **-Psalm 119:105**

> *The entrance of thy words giveth light;*
> *it giveth understanding unto the simple.*
> **-Psalm 119:130**

---

[1] All Scripture quotations are taken from the King James Version (KJV) unless otherwise stated.

~ 1 ~

THE IMPORTANCE OF SPIRITUAL SUBSTANCE

Encouragement with no substance eventually results in death. Why is this statement so important as it relates to our wellbeing? An example would be a hyperventilating, long-distance runner dying of thirst. The crowd and the coach encourage and empower the athlete to finish the race. He is motivated by their cheers, giving him enough push to get to the finish line. The question is, *despite the loud cheers, is he still dying?* Does his body still need the essential nutrients to help support his wellbeing? The answer is *yes*! Although he has made it to the finish line, he still needs substances, such as water, salt, and electrolytes, to refuel and replenish his lost nutrients. These are the very substances causing his body to die and his life to slip away. While he's thankful for the cheers and support from his coach, he still needs to consume these essential nutrients.

Likewise, our spirit and soul still need God's Word, which is the substance of our being. Matthew 5:6 states, "Blessed are they who do hunger and thirst after righteousness: for they shall be filled." The Lord still sends us exhortation in times of trouble, but His Word of instruction and correction is the substance for our soul. Our faith must be fueled by the Word of truth so that those who follow the way may endure the test of time.

> *Now faith is the substance of things hoped for, the evidence of things not seen.*
> **-Hebrews 11:1**

The substance of the Word fuels our faith, and our faith only increases when the truth of the Word infills our souls.

Preachers often believe that pumping up and priming the congregation is enough to save their souls, but it's not. The flock of famishing and wandering sheep must be fed the Word of God. Pumping and priming help people in the short run, but the sound teaching of God's Word will save their souls in the long run, delivering them from their transgressive ways.

In John 21:15-17, Jesus (Yeshua) Christ charges Simon Peter to feed His lambs and sheep, a true expression of love and dedication. Mark 4:14 states, "The sower sows the word." The Word is more important than riches and fame because it converts the soul unto righteousness so that those who receive may be fed and inherit eternal life.

Thank God for His Word, our essential substance, because it directs us in the *way* of Christ and unto God's eternal salvation through His Son. Amen!

~ 2 ~

JUDGMENT ON THE UNRULY SHEEP

A sheep that doesn't desire to follow its shepherd should no longer be a part of the flock, nor should it be allowed to graze in the pasture. The evil intentions of the sheep warrants a spiritual conviction, but judicial or political consequences cannot be administered without physical action/causation. Matthew 15:19 states, "For out of the heart proceed evil thoughts, murders, adulteries, fornications, thefts, false witness, blasphemies." The shepherd's job is to do his best to keep the sheep in the fold. If the decision made by the sheep is folly, the shepherd should allow the sheep to wander off into the wilderness. John 10:25-29 states the following:

> *Jesus answered them, I told you, and ye believed not: the works that I do in my Father's name, they bear witness of me. But ye believe not, because ye are not of my sheep, as I said unto you. My sheep hear my voice, and I know them, and they follow me: And I give unto them eternal life; and they shall never perish, neither shall, any man pluck them out of my hand. My Father, which gave them me, is greater than all; and no man is able to pluck them out of my Father's hand.*

This sheep is *not* lost because he *consciously* chose to defy the command of the good shepherd by denying His voice.

If such a sheep remain in the flock after committing continuous acts of treason, the other sheep will, in turn, be exposed to his negative influence and defy the shepherd and turn away from the flock. As the old saying goes, *one bad apple can contaminate the whole bunch.*

Certain people in our lives must be removed that may have an involuntary influence on our lives without our knowledge. There also may be specific characteristics within us that are genetic in origin or spiritual in which we have to be purged. No matter the case, we need to be loosed from the seed of wickedness that has been sowed in our subconscious minds.

May the power of Christ transform us daily until we are made utterly pure from all unrighteousness.

> *Casting down imaginations, and every high thing that exalteth itself against the knowledge of God, and bringing into captivity every thought to the obedience of Christ.*
> **-2 Corinthians 10:5**

~ 3 ~

BE HUMBLE AND FEARLESS

Humble yourselves therefore under the mighty hand of God, that he may exalt you in due time.
-1 Peter 5:6

This scripture is very profound in its descriptive assertion of how God protects those who humble themselves before Him. It further indicates that God, in His infinite wisdom, understands when is the best time to exalt those who are spiritually and physically submissive. We often try to do things on our own and in our strength to push the will of God faster than needed, and this is an attitude of impudence, folly, and impatience caused by fear and doubt.

Some believers even become cowardly on the battlefield, causing them to commit ungodly treason and break their covenant vows. Doesn't this sound hypocritical in its context? And we have to ask ourselves, *even in God's infinite love towards us, does He love a cowardly soldier that professes they have faith before men but plots betrayal in their dungeons of secrecy?* Revelation 21:8 states, "But the fearful, and unbelieving, and the abominable, and murderers, and whoremongers, and sorcerers, and idolaters, and all liars, shall have their part in the lake which burneth with fire and brimstone: which is the second death." Can a man hide from God? Can he retract his shadow from the light of the sun without being seen? Are our actions hidden before the Lord of hosts? Even our enemies will know of our cowardness.

What did the Lord warn Jeremiah about concerning this very spirit? Jeremiah 1:17 states, "Thou therefore gird up thy loins, and arise, and speak unto them all that I command thee: be not dismayed at their faces, lest I confound thee before them." Fearlessness is required. Who should we fear according to God's Word? Matthew 10:28 states, "And fear not them which kill the body, but are not able to kill the soul: but rather fear him which is able to destroy both soul and body in hell." God puts a major emphasis on humility and fearlessness, even to the point where He encourages us to resist Satan:

> But he giveth more grace. Wherefore he saith, God resisteth the proud, but giveth grace unto the humble. Submit yourselves therefore to God. Resist the devil, and he will flee from you.
> *-James 4:6-7*

God is asking who will be fearless and stand: "Who will rise up for me against the evildoers? or who will stand up for me against the workers of iniquity?" (Psalm 94:16). In 1 Corinthians 16:13, He encourages us: "Watch, stand fast in the faith, be brave, be strong."

> *And he said to them all, If any man will come after me, let him deny himself, and take up his cross daily, and follow me. For whosoever will save his life shall lose it: but whosoever will lose his life for my sake, the same shall save it.*
> **-Luke 9:23-24**

See brethren, there is no merit in being a coward, and there is no reward for denying your faith in Christ. Such behavior will only result in a dishonorable discharge. So I beseech you, brethren in Christ, to walk in the Spirit in order not to indulge in the passions of the flesh. Be strong, courageous, and prayerful, knowing your righteous reward is in heaven.

May the Father in heaven strengthen you, and may the Word of God (His Son) show you the Way. God bless!

~ 4 ~

MEAT THAT NOURISHES THE SOUL

> And that from a child thou hast known the holy scriptures, which are able to make thee wise unto salvation through faith which is in Christ Jesus. All scripture is given by inspiration of God, and is profitable for doctrine, for reproof, for correction, for instruction in righteousness: That the man of God may be perfect, thoroughly furnished unto all good works.
> **-2 Timothy 3:15-17**

All meat does not nourish the soul or bring enlightenment to the body. The meat of the Spirit is the Word of God, and His righteousness is to be consumed. Only sound doctrine is to be consumed by, especially, those who have been set apart by grace as vessels of God, the Father, and His Christ.

Brethren, be mindful because there is a barrage of witnesses monitoring your actions; be careful of your living so that your acts of righteousness may not be in vain but identified by Christ Yeshua before the Lord of Glory, our Father who art in Heaven.

Do all creatures require the same nutrition to sustain their biological forms, or do all beings drink the same formula for sustenance? No, yet nature is attracted to what is customary for their survival and the building of their temples. So we, as believers, must likewise do the same. Do herbivores and carnivores consume the same meat? Or does one consume the meat of plants and the other the meat of animals? We, who are advocates of righteousness and ambassadors of the Kingdom of our God, must consume the meat of Truth to keep our flesh subjugated to produce fruit of the Spirit. Galatians 5:22-23 states, "But the fruit of the Spirit is love, joy, peace, longsuffering, gentleness, goodness, faith, meekness, temperance: against such, there is no law." We are both spiritual and physical beings created by the Most High God. Are we to feed one and neglect the other? Are we to feed only the spirit and deprive the physical body of nourishment? 1 Peter 2:2 states, "Like newborn babies, long for the pure milk of the word, so that by it you may grow in respect to salvation" (NIV). What are the results of neglecting the spirit man? Such actions of depravity will only result in an internal imbalance of the subconscious mind.

Let us be complementary to good works and uncompromising in our journey of enlightenment that we may be examples to future generations as Christ is unto us.

Be blessed faithful servants of God, the Father, and Christ Yeshua, our Lord. Amen!

> Now then we are ambassadors for Christ, as though God did beseech you by us: we pray you in Christ's stead, be ye reconciled to God.
> **-2 Corinthians 5:20**

~ 5 ~

GOD AS YOUR SUPPLIER

But my God shall supply all your needs according to his riches in glory by Christ Jesus.
-**Philippians 4:19**

When a manufacturer or producer is in a business relationship with a distributor or retailer, they generally agree to a particular product sold on the market that both the producer and seller can benefit from monetarily. Usually, what needs to be supplied is already in stock or doesn't take much time to produce. So when God's Word reveals His ability to supply our needs through Christ, that tells the believer two things: it's already in stock, or it won't take too long to manifest. One thing is sure; having God as our supplier ensures us that our needs will be delivered without fail.

Problems occur spiritually and physically due to living in an imperfect material world; however, any good business will guarantee satisfaction and fulfill its obligations. If interference happens where it seems like they can't deliver on time, then that business or company will make compensation for your troubles. Like in the case of Job, God will give you double for your trouble.

Job 42:10 states, "And the Lord turned the captivity of Job, when he prayed for his friends: also the Lord gave Job twice as much as he had before." Just like Daniel, who was in distress due to a vision He had, despite the seemingly extensive delay to his prayer concerning the vision, the Angel of the Lord let the troubled prophet know that God heard him the moment he began praying and fasting:

> *Fear not, Daniel, for from the first day that thou didst set thine heart to understand and to chasten thyself before thy God, thy words were heard; and I have come for thy words.*
> **-Daniel 10:12**

He also informed Daniel about the supernatural events that caused the delay, enhancing Daniel's wisdom, understanding, and relationship with God:

> *But the prince of the kingdom of Persia withstood me one and twenty days: but, lo, Michael, one of the chief princes, came to help me; and I remained there with the kings of Persia. Now I am come to make thee understand what shall befall thy people in the latter days: for yet the vision is for many days.*
> **-Daniel 10:13-14**

So don't worry about when the package will arrive; just know that God always shows up right on time for His beloved people who put their faith and trust in Him. For it is written: trust in the

Lord with all thy heart and lean not unto your understanding, acknowledge Him in all you do, and He will direct your paths (Proverbs 3:5-6).

Hallelujah to the Most High God and unto the Lamb.

~ 6 ~

UNDERSTANDING THE WAR WITHIN

Inner warfare, which inhabits a person's mind, is mental and spiritual. Psychological trauma may be a genetic predisposition that requires healing through the spirit of counsel. It's never our intention to be a certain way, but the Spirit of the Lord has to remove this genetic inclination to display specific behavior that may even cause confusion.

Bad behavior results from generational curses that are scientifically proven to be spiritual. Trauma can attach itself to your DNA as a memory, and one must fight to remove the evil force from within themselves so one will not pass it down from generation to generation. But God's Love gives us direction through his Word. It is written that perfect love removes all fear, and love covers or eliminates many sins (1 John 4:18). Love conquers all and removes the limitations of genetic predisposition. That means you were already genetically predisposed to specific behavioral characteristics. So the only way to overcome sin and generational curses are through God's perfect love. Remember whom the Son sets free is truly free indeed.

This was Paul's display of a faithful witness and confession before God and man:

> For that which I do I allow not: for what I would, that do I not; but what I hate, that do I. If then I do that which I would not, I consent unto the law that it is good. Now then, it is no more I that do it, but sin that dwelleth in me. For I know that in me (that is, in my flesh) dwelleth no good thing: for to will is present with me; but how to perform that which is good I find not. For the good that I would I do not: but the evil I would not, that I do. Now, if I do that I would not; it is no more I that do it, but sin that dwelleth in me.
> **-Romans 7:15-20**

Consent to understand one's faults and physical limitations that the Lord may command His Spirit to help you in your weakness:

> For this thing, I sought the Lord thrice, that it might depart from me. And he said unto me, My grace is sufficient for thee: for my strength is made perfect in weakness. Most gladly, therefore, will I rather glory in my infirmities, that the power of Christ may rest upon me. Therefore I take pleasure in infirmities, in reproaches, in necessities, in persecutions, in distresses for Christ's sake: for when I am weak, then am I strong.
> **-2 Corinthians 12:8-10**

~ 7 ~

RELATIONSHIP BETWEEN A KING AND HIS WIFE

    How does a genuine king gain respect from his royal subjects and people? He must understand roles and gifts, and his heart should be committed to the Lord. He shouldn't be as Ahab, who allowed his idol-worshipping wife, Jezebel, to manipulate him and take Him away from his foundation in God. A king's wife should always be in spiritual agreement with him as long as he remains principled and disciplined in his practice. For it will be the Lord, the God of Israel, the God of Heaven and Earth who exalts him and anoints him. And a godly man should desire a praying wife, a wife that's willing to protect and cover his soul (even the gift that God has blessed him with to rule). She must fully accept her skill, her position in Christ, and deny herself to walk with Christ and in the power of the Holy Spirit. For it is written, a wife is a gift from God, and a man that finds a wife finds a good thing and obtains favor from God (Proverbs 18:22).

    1 Peter 3:4 states, "But let it be the hidden man of the heart, in that which is not corruptible, even the ornament of a meek and quiet spirit, which is in the sight of God of great price." So when wives are under attack and feel defeated in godly

relationships, it's because God has put a good thing on the inside of them for His purpose. Her husband, an ambassador of Christ, protects and endows her with gifts because of her faithfulness. I strongly desire to encourage wives in the faith not to be cut off, removed, and cast into the furnace, like a branch. The branch no longer bears fruit, but it still absorbs the moisture and nutrients from the other stalks; however, it hinders them from producing more fruit.

> *Every branch in me that beareth not fruit he taketh away: and every branch that beareth fruit, he purgeth it, that it may bring forth more fruit. Now ye are clean through the word which I have spoken unto you.*
> **-John 15:2-3**

In all things, protect your family with prayer, even pray over your household and anoint your doorpost. The Word says to pray without ceasing. And after you've given your all in worship, glorify God.

To all my brothers and sisters in Christ, I salute you in the name of Christ. Be blessed!

~ 8 ~

THE POWER OF A WILL TO CHANGE

Never allow the destructive will of another man's lifestyle to affect your walk with Christ. The decision to covet another man's possessions may deter us from our destiny. We cannot forget the effects our choices and decisions have on others' ability to maneuver in this life:

> *Wherefore seeing we also are compassed about with so great a cloud of witnesses, let us lay aside every weight, and the sin which doth so easily beset us, and let us run with patience the race set before us.*
> **-Hebrews 12:1**

This text implies that people who look up to us as positive role models tend to model their character and actions after our own. Romans 12:21 states, "Be not overcome with evil, but overcome evil with good." It is also written not to allow your good to be evil spoken of (Romans 14:16).

As the saying goes, *if you put a seed into the ground, that's the harvest you're going to get in due season based on that seed's identity.* So we have to be careful what seeds we sow into ourselves and others. Most people don't change within themselves, but they may respond to the change within another person. If your change is a greater force than their change, they are more likely to subject themselves to that greater force of will.

For whatsoever is born of God overcometh the world: this is the victory that overcometh the world, even our faith.
-1 John 5:4

A vicious dog trained to attack off of instinct will carefully guard its master's possessions, but that dog will never attack his master due to reverential fear. That same instinctive characteristic respectfully recognizes its relationship with that individual. This is what we gain through Christ—the innate spiritual ability to subjugate demons and evil forces. These forces may not change their character or nature, but the authority of Christ through the power of the Holy Spirit will cause them to recognize the change in us.

Therefore if any man be in Christ, he is a new creature: old things are passed away; behold, all things are become new.
-2 Corinthians 5:17

Do not conform to the patterns of this world; instead, be transformed by the renewing of your mind.
-Romans 8:37

A change or transformation requires a process: a state of metamorphosis.
Brethren, let God transform your life! Amen.

Nay, in all these things, we are more than conquerors through him that loved us.
Romans 8:37

~ 9 ~

THE IMAGE OF GOD CAN BE RESTORED

Sin destroys the image of God. Sin is not just a term illustrating error; it is an action that causes error to occur. It is performed over and over again, giving off the impression of insanity. Sinning is a process of continuous disobedience that causes an individual to miss the mark of their responsibility (calling or purpose).

> *Whosoever committeth sin transgresseth also the law: for sin is the transgression of the law.*
> *-1 John 3:4*

Sin is not a feeling of lust; it is an action caused by a strong desire and a carnal mind (perverted mindset). It is the manifestation of self-interest being performed outside of the will of the Spirit. Galatians 5:16 states, "This I say then, Walk in the Spirit, and ye shall not fulfill the lust of the flesh." Sometimes we can believe that we have thought something through without realizing the imperfections of our cognitive decisions (a decision performed in our minds first and something we imagined to be correct without knowing it to be conceived in error). Romans 7:25 states, "I thank God through Jesus Christ our Lord. So then with the mind, I myself serve the law of God; but with the flesh the law of sin." The Lord understands imperfections in the flesh, but He doesn't allow those imperfections to become an excuse. God gives us the ability to control or exercise self-control over ourselves through faith and willpower. He gives us the Spirit to overcome our physical and emotional imperfections. Matthew 26:41 states, "Watch and pray, that ye enter not into temptation: the spirit indeed is willing, but the flesh is weak." We can choose to tap into the strength He has offered us as an investment. It isn't to do what we want to do with it in our lust, but it's to use it for His glory with the provision of instructions. If someone is hired to do a job, are instructions not provided on how it should be done? If they violate those instructions, the immediate consequence is usually to terminate the individual in question after careful consideration. They broke the agreement, so the employer had to let them go. Emotions were not involved because the primary goal was to take care of business. Deuteronomy 28:1 states, "And it shall come to pass, if thou shalt hearken diligently unto the voice of the Lord thy God, to observe and to do all his commandments which I command thee this day, that the Lord thy God will set thee on high above all nations of the earth." Lust (a cause of sin) causes us to violate the agreement we have with our employer (in this case, God). Before we do anything additional, we must consult with the employer to get their allowance if the proposition is beneficial. God is strategic and wise, so He commits Himself to do things a certain way to create structure in the universe.

Sin goes against God's original plan; even if evil and chaos exist, God still has to be consulted about decisions. Isaiah 45:7 states, "I form the light, and create darkness: I make peace, and create evil: I the Lord do all these things." Relationships work better when all individuals are operating on one accord. Don't allow your impulsive lusts to cause you to sin against the Eternal God and your soul. Put your lust under subjection by the Word of God and the Spirit of the Most High. What used to be abstract comes into being when God orders it to be so. Whether we understand it or not, we need to comply with the intent of learning from God to better ourselves and others around us. 1 Corinthians 9:27, "But I keep under my body, and bring it into subjection: lest that by any means, when I have preached to others, I myself should be a castaway." Remember, God is not a man, so He doesn't function like a man. Numbers 23:19 states, "God is not a man, that he should lie; neither the son of man, that he should repent: hath he said, and shall he not do it? or hath he spoken, and shall he not make it good?" This is the reason they didn't accept Christ because they couldn't conceptualize His functionality enough to control Him. What He had on the inside of Him was too significant for them to contain, so He broke free whenever they tried to restrain Him. Lust couldn't hold Him down, hunger couldn't persuade Him, women couldn't manipulate Him, death couldn't consume Him, and the grave couldn't keep Him prisoner. Christ broke free, not with His flesh, but with what was on the inside. He said, when you see me, you see my Father in Heaven, the Eternal God in His physical form. And God, in His great nature (Spirit and discipline), causes worldly lusts to flee from His presence.

1 Corinthians 15:50 says, "Now this I say, brethren, that flesh and blood cannot inherit the kingdom of God; neither doth

corruption inherit incorruption." So don't worry about what happens to your flesh; always govern the actions of your spirit (your inner man). Don't allow sin to destroy the image that God has given you. While growing up, you can say that you didn't have the privilege of knowing God, so your morals were somewhat suppressed. Well, that's an acceptable excuse, but God can restore those who desire to be made over and made whole. For it is written: He leads me beside the still waters, and He restores my soul (Psalm 23:2-3). The very things and people who helped destroy your image, in your ignorance, can be removed from your life for a season or period so God can transform you back into the image He originally designed you to have.

Become a new creature through Christ, Yeshua. May God receive all the honor and all the glory forever and ever. Amen!

~ 10 ~

SEASON FOR PLANTING

To everything, there is a season and a time to every purpose under the heaven.
-Ecclesiastes 3:1

There is a season for planting and transplanting an individual organism in a new location. When a plant first begins, it is fragile, needs careful attention, and must be watered and nurtured at a certain rate. Sometimes, the plant has to start on the inside before being exposed to the outside elements. When a plant has been cultivated to a certain height or level on the inside, eventually, it has to be moved on the outside to a climate more befitting for its potential growth. The plant was too weak on its own to survive before, but the gardener or caretaker had to release the plant to the outside to grow. On the inside, the plant didn't require much discipline, but once it was moved to the outside, it had to make an innate decision to adapt to the new environment. The plant had to remember that it was made for the outside even though it started inside. Now, it can begin the process of existential growth. Genesis 1:11-12 says, "And God said, Let the earth bring forth grass, the herb yielding seed, and the fruit tree yielding fruit after his kind, whose seed is in itself, upon the earth: and it was so. And the earth brought forth grass, and herb yielding seed after his kind, and the tree yielding fruit, whose seed was in itself, after his kind: and God saw that it was good." Just like the plant, we as believers and followers of Christ have to be moved from our old environment to grow.

The discipline of God started on the inside, but now, God has to move us outside of our comfort zone. The Word is sent forth to test us as capable vessels for the presence of the Most High God. Deuteronomy 32:2 states, "Let my teaching drop as the rain, My speech distill as the dew, As raindrops on the tender herb, And as showers on the grass" (NKJV). The will of the believer has to be tested. We are the same plant God nurtured in Spirit, yet we have been moved to a larger environment. God desires to move us to a higher level and larger environment, but we must be ready. Acts 3:19 says, "Repent ye therefore, and be converted, that your sins may be blotted out, when the times of refreshing shall come from the presence of the Lord." If He moves us too fast, without preparation, we will spiritually die before we ascend to our new level of consciousness. God will prepare you, and He will move you in due time and due season.

And let us not be weary in doing well: for in due season we shall reap if we faint not.
-Galatians 6:9

Brethren, be patient in faith and instant in prayer. All praise to the Most High through His Christ. Amen!

~ 11 ~

IMPURITIES OF TODAY'S KNOWLEDGE

But thou, O Daniel, shut up the words, and seal the book, even to the time of the end: many shall run to and fro, and knowledge shall be increased.
-*Daniel 12:4*

How much information is too much information? Our generation is lost from a compilation of subconscious variables caused by an influx of information. The idea of having too much information is bad depending on what's resourceful for growth, and the idea of not having enough information is terrible depending on what's lacking as a necessity. A container can only hold up to the capacity in which it is designed to hold. This generation is lost under the rubble of knowledge and information guided by social media, technology, television, the internet, cellular devices, and vain knowledge. Degenerate books are available to teens who don't have the means to attain a driver's license independently. Yet, they read the vulgarity introduced by inhumane authors and publishers (including certain religious ideas and philosophies).

Knowledge has become an uncontrollable force and a poison to the youth. What does the Word speak concerning knowledge? 1 Corinthians 3:19-20 states, "For the wisdom of this world is foolishness with God. For it is written, He taketh the wise in their own craftiness. And again, The Lord knoweth the thoughts of the wise, that they are vain." James 3:17 states, "But the wisdom that is from above is first pure, then peaceable, gentle, and easy to be intreated, full of mercy and good fruits, without partiality, and without hypocrisy." Good and evil are substances that the wisdom of God can only control. So, what is actually hurting our society as a whole? Well, all has been revealed in God's Word of truth of what was, is, and is to come.

Without God, we are lost, hopeless relics seeking to be found. The only known way to be released from the bondage of impure knowledge is to forget what we thought we knew and learn of God. Matthew 11:28-30 says, "Come unto me, all ye that labor and are heavily laden, and I will give you rest. Take my yoke upon you, and learn of me; for I am meek and lowly in heart: and ye shall find rest unto your souls. For my yoke is easy, and my burden is light." Emptying ourselves is the only way to be truly enlightened. God cleanses through words of correction and with a rod of truth and salvation.

Now ye are clean through the word which I have spoken unto you. Abide in me, and I in you. As the branch cannot bear fruit of itself, except it abide in the vine; no more can ye, except ye abide in me. I am the vine, ye are the branches: He that abideth in me, and I in him, the same bringeth forth much fruit: for without me ye can do nothing.
-**John 15:3-5**

Brethren, be purified and transformed through God's Word by the inner workings of His Spirit. May the Most High and His Christ be glorified forever. Amen!

~ 12 ~

THE WAR BETWEEN WANTS AND NEEDS

But my God shall supply all your need according to his riches in glory by Christ Jesus.
-Philippians 4:19

Wants can wait; needs are now. Both are desires, but which is more significant (a need or a want)? Which desire does the living God respond to most among His people, even the whole earth? Did He send His Son because we wanted Him as a sacred possession, or did He send Christ because we needed Him for the salvation of our souls?

For God so loved the world, that he gave his only begotten Son, that whosoever believeth in him should not perish, but have everlasting life.
-John 3:16

The Lord always prioritizes the need in our situations. The flesh is wicked beyond reason. There is an uncontrollable urge that spawns from within our hearts, even to the point where the lust of this world would overtake us apart from Christ and God's grace. So the need becomes more of a focus than the want, yet God still doesn't desire for us to dwell on the need itself. In Him, we lack nothing (Psalm 23:1). Acts 17:28 says, "For in him we live, and move, and have our being; as certain also of your own poets have said, For we are also his offspring." If we are considered the offspring of the Eternal Father, why wouldn't He provide for His obedient children? Matthew 7:11 says, "If ye then, being evil, know how to give good gifts unto your children, how much more shall your Father which is in heaven give good things to them that ask him?" God doesn't desire us to focus on wants because wants can become lustful desires which can lead to sin. Make your requests known to the Lord and let go because in Him are all things and for Him, all things are created. If we abide in Him, we can access what belongs to God and what we need.

How much do we lack in want relative to what we lack in need? Life is about maturity. We water plants based on the nutrition needed to grow and produce in their season. Is water not a need rather than a want? Philippians 4:11-12 says, "Not that I speak in respect of want: for I have learned, in whatsoever state I am, therewith to be content. I know both how to be abased, and I know how to abound: everywhere and in all things, I am instructed both to be full and to be hungry, both to abound and to suffer need." How do we satisfy the needs of our souls and the desire of our spirit that the inner man may be filled? The Word says in Psalm 107:9, "For he satisfieth the longing soul, and filleth the hungry soul with goodness." John 6:35 says, "And Jesus said unto them, I am the bread of life: he that cometh to me shall never hunger; and he that believeth on me shall never thirst."

An apparent implication is placed on an intangible longing that Christ can only satisfy.

Unless we, as followers of Christ, put on His person, our spiritual essence will never be replenished, and in turn, we shall forever suffer a need the world could never fill.

> *I have been young, and now am old; yet have I not seen the righteous forsaken, nor his seed begging bread.*
> **-Psalm 37:25**

Brethren, let God supply your needs so that you may truly be filled. Amen.

~ 13 ~

HOW TO DISCERN SPIRITUAL ENERGY AND DEFEAT GLUTTONY

If you hang around someone long enough, you will imitate their bad habits. This includes the energy they emit and certain things they consume or overindulge in. Can energy have a negative impact on marriage? If the answer is *yes*, what type of energy is considered toxic? The most challenging thing in marriage is being connected to an individual and drawing in their emotional energies but not knowing their emotions' effects on you. Energy attracts energy, and energy feeds on energy to sustain itself. If there is negative energy around, most people will feed on negative energy. However, if positive energy is nearby, that is the energy source to be consumed because it's more beneficial to the soul.

How does the enemy use negative energy to cause chaos in relationships? Emotional turmoil is a tactic of the enemy used to subjugate the spirit man to the will of the flesh. A man in control of his spirit can govern and takedown major cities: "He that is slow to anger is better than the mighty, and he that ruleth his spirit than he that taketh a city" (Proverbs 16:32).

What I've found to be amazing is that the food choices we consume play a significant role in our choices concerning spiritual growth. When you are spiritually connected to someone, you can pick up on their mood changes. And we all know that overeating is considered gluttony (a capital vice). If your brain is deprived of good-quality nutrition, or if free radicals or damaging inflammatory cells are circulating within the brain's enclosed space, further contributing to brain tissue injury, consequences are to be expected. When you eat clean, you feel better, and eating proportionally also plays a role in bio-energy regulation in the body.

Did Christ have to overcome the spirit of gluttony to enhance his spiritual anointing? Christ went into the wilderness to defeat the spirit of overconsumption (gluttony) by entirely relying on the Word of God:

> *And when the tempter came to him, he said If thou be the Son of God, command that these stones be made bread. But he answered and said, It is written, Man shall not live by bread alone, but by every word that proceedeth out of the mouth of God.*
> **-Matthew 4:3-4**

I've been guilty of overconsumption myself, and in terms of mood, overconsumption can cause one to become more irritable and wrathful. When Satan attempted to tempt Christ in the wilderness, what was His primary focus? It was a particular food selection that people in that day were accustomed to eating (bread). Satan told Christ, if He was the Son of God, turn the stones into bread. He attempted to play on his ego while Christ was in a weakened state. Christ replied by saying, Man shall not live by bread (food) alone, but by every Word (scripture) that proceeds out of the mouth of God, the Father.

The liberal soul shall be made fat: and he that watereth shall be watered also himself.
-Proverbs 11:25

Let's take a lesson from Christ and allow the Spirit of God to help us take back control of our bodies from Satan. Be blessed!

~ 14 ~

OBSTACLES ENCOUNTERED DURING A MAJOR TRANSITION

We encounter some of the most significant obstacles in our lives when we are in the process of a major transition. A transition can hurt, whether it's a transformation or relocation. It will either make you or break you. However, major transitions can be endured more efficiently by submitting fully to the Holy Spirit. In this world, obstacles are allowed to happen so that our faith may be strengthened in the way of righteousness and so that God may be glorified.

In a transition state, it can make you feel like everything possible is waging war against you. Even when you pray or seek God intently, it can feel like there is no change. If there is evidence of change, you still must hold it together throughout the process.

The most important part of a healthy transition is letting go of the old to incorporate the new. Many things must die: old habits, situations you used to be involved in, old relationships, your old way of thinking, and overall, the old you. It can be challenging to overcome these situations on your own without the power of God, through Christ, but you still must believe based on what God has revealed to you.

When you're faced with impossible situations, that's when you must give all to God after you've done all you can to stand. No matter your level of faith, love, or spirituality, you still need help through these transitions.

One of the most challenging aspects of a transition is when you must endure the process while connected to others who don't understand your transition or call. Trying to fit them into an invaluable equation is complicated and sometimes virtually impossible. That's when you have to remember God's Word and stand on God's Word while canceling out what others have to say about you. For example, when God is declaring your confidence, jealous spirits will speak pride over your life simply because you love God to the point of allowing His Spirit to seal His commandments upon your heart and transform you. So, the only identifiable element in that transition is the self. Self-analyzation is the key. If one cannot identify with self intently based on what the Spirit of God reveals, they will not acquire the necessary tools to evolve or help others. Here's a word of caution: you must understand that many people detest or hate when you're trying to identify with yourself.

> *And why beholdest thou the mote that is in thy brother's eye, but considerest not the beam that is in thine own eye? Or how wilt thou say to thy brother, Let me pull the mote out of thine eye; and, behold, a beam is in thine own eye? Thou hypocrite, first cast out the beam out of thine own eye; and then shalt thou see clearly to cast out the mote out of thy brother's eye.*
> *-Matthew 7:3-5*

Only the Spirit of Truth can help and motivate us to see ourselves. Some will fight against such a revelation, but if it's according to the will of God, they will eventually submit to the truth. That acceptance is the beginning of their transformation, which is notably one of the most significant transitions of their lives.

Brethren, let's aim for authenticity, boldness, truth, love, peace, longsuffering, patience, empathy, confidence, self-analyzation, and purity so that we may be made true manifested sons of God through His Spirit and by Christ Yeshua.

Therefore if any man is in Christ, he is a new creature: old things are passed away; behold, all things have become new. And all things are of God, who hath reconciled us to himself by Jesus Christ, and hath given to us the ministry of reconciliation; To wit, that God was in Christ, reconciling the world unto himself, not imputing their trespasses unto them; and hath committed unto us the word of reconciliation. Now then we are ambassadors for Christ, as though God did beseech you by us: we pray you in Christ's stead, be ye reconciled to God. For he hath made him be sin for us, who knew no sin; that we might be made the righteousness of God in him.
-2 Corinthians 5:17-21

~ 15 ~

WHEN THE LORD TRANSPLANTS YOU IN A NEW ENVIRONMENT

Those that be planted in the house of the Lord shall flourish in the courts of our God. They shall still bring forth fruit in old age; they shall be fat and flourishing; To shew that the Lord is upright: he is my rock, and there is no unrighteousness in him.
-Psalm 92:13-15

When a farmer transplants a tree, it goes into shock. So, what process should the tree go through in preparation for transplanting? Should the farmer concern himself with preserving the tree during the transplantation process at all? Well, the most critical factor relating to trees is that trees are living organisms, so they should be handled with care.

The first thing to remember is that when one is transplanting a tree, one is taking it out of the environment that it's accustomed to. Remember that just because you're accustomed to something doesn't always mean you're comfortable. All farmers must remember this when handling newly matured trees.

Now to answer how farmers should prepare trees for transplanting: trees should be watered and fed essential nutrients before being transplanted. Their roots and limbs should be adequately secure and tied together delicately to avoid breakage. Remember that the roots are the anchor and foundation of a vascular plant (including trees). This is where water and nutrients are absorbed into the plant from the soil. So, if the tree is not handled appropriately before being transplanted, it will die before it even makes it into its new environment.

Let's analyze the shocking process and why trees, like other plants, experience shock. First of all, what is *shock*? Shock is when plants are moved suddenly without sufficient nutrients to carry them into their following environment. Without these essential nutrients, plants cannot handle the shift or relocation.

Now, how does God relate us to plants or nature? And can these same conditions affect us during transitional periods within our lives? Well, let's see what the Word of God says concerning us being planted or moved:

And he shall be like a tree planted by the rivers of water, that bringeth forth his fruit in his season; his leaf also shall not wither, and whatsoever he doeth shall prosper.
-Psalm 1:3

So, this passage of scripture states that God will plant His righteous servant or people like a tree by the water. See, the sovereign Lord doesn't just plant us anywhere. He plants us where we can grow and expand to new levels or new heights. He plants us where we can receive nourishment and substance. He plants us where we can prosper and bear fruit even as our souls prosper. When a tree begins to die, God sends rain from the heavens. When we start to die in our current situations before a transition, God sends us the nourishment of His Spirit. These are the benefits of those who serve the Lord with their whole heart and are declared righteous according to His Word.

Brethren, delight yourself in the Lord and meditate on His Word to be planted and flourish. Amen.

Let my teaching drop as the rain, My speech distills as the dew, As the droplets on the fresh grass And as the showers on the herb.
-Deuteronomy 32:2

~ 16 ~

STANDING IN THE FACE OF ADVERSITY

Is facing adversity necessary, and why does it seem like God allows people close to us to be a part of that process? More importantly, how should we handle ourselves when we are frustrated with God and the process that He allows us to transition through? It is written: A friend loves at all times, and a brother is born for adversity (Proverbs 17:17). So, the Word is telling us that friends and brethren are there with us amid our trials and tribulations, either as a means of moral and spiritual support or as a minister of opposition.

As believers or followers of Christ, we must endure the process, whatever the case may be. James 1:3 tells us that the testing of our faith produces endurance. Sometimes you must understand why you face the adversity that the Lord allows you to go through, and if you lack understanding, ask your generous Father who is in heaven. For it is written in James 1:5, "If any of you lack wisdom, let him ask of God, that giveth to all men liberally, and upbraideth not; and it shall be given him." How you make it through your process depends upon you and your mindset. A healthy perspective helps us endure in times of great hardship. Throughout the hurt, the heartache, trials, and tribulations, know that God still loves you. However, He hates wickedness, so He presents us with a choice to define our relationship with Him. Psalm 37:28-29 states, "For the Lord loveth judgment, and forsaketh, not his saints; they are preserved forever: but the seed of the wicked shall be cut off. The righteous shall inherit the land, and dwell therein forever." This is why the Word says obedience is greater than sacrifice. Throughout all the sacrifices you make, you have to ask yourself if you were obedient to God's instructions. Did you take the time to hear Him, or did you act on impulse? Hebrews 3:15 states, "Today if ye will hear his voice, harden not your hearts, as in the provocation" (a period in which Israel provoked the Lord to wrath). Did you feel the Lord was taking too long, or were you angry that things weren't going your way? Self-reflection is the key to growth and spiritual enlightenment; be sure that your emotions don't consume you.

What does the Most High say in regards to observing His instructions? Deuteronomy 28:1-2 answers, "And it shall come to pass, if thou shalt hearken diligently unto the voice of the Lord thy God, to observe and to do all his commandments which I command thee this day, that the Lord thy God will set thee on high above all nations of the earth: And all these blessings shall come on thee, and overtake thee if thou shalt hearken unto the voice of the Lord thy God." Will God's instructions not guide us during our test? The Kingdom of God isn't just handed to any of us on a silver platter. We must earn our way by keeping His commandments. Verify what His commandments are by observing His Word and see if our thoughts and opinions align or if we're in opposition to His way.

Most people who live in sin hate the Word of truth because it reveals their innermost issues; a true believer openly accepts their conviction and apply the Word to correct what was once in error. 2 Timothy 3:16-17 states, "All scripture is given by inspiration of God, and is profitable for doctrine, for reproof, for correction, for instruction in righteousness: That the man of God may be perfect, thoroughly furnished unto all good works." None of us can control the lives or actions of others, but we can take time to develop ourselves. So, before we begin to analyze others, please look within to allow the Word of the Most High to help us repair our brokenness. Each one of us must suffer our own judgment, especially when we're outside of the will of God. The Lord will keep taking you through until you realign yourself with Him according to His righteousness.

Brethren, stand in the face of adversity with the Word of God as your sword. Be a conqueror. All praise to the Most High God! Amen.

> And why beholdest thou the mote that is in thy brother's eye, but considerest not the beam that is in thine own eye? Or how wilt thou say to thy brother, Let me pull the mote out of thine eye; and, behold, a beam is in thine own eye? Thou hypocrite, first cast out the beam out of thine own eye; and then shalt thou see clearly to cast out the mote out of thy brother's eye.
> **-Matthew 7:3-5**

~ 17 ~

CANCELING OUT NEGATIVITY

> *Keep a good conscience so that in the thing in which you are slandered, those who revile your good behavior in Christ will be put to shame.*
> **-1 Peter 3:16**

Can producing a negative mindset destroy a good conscience? Negativity can cause cancer, so stop being negative. Impatience induces stress which causes cancerous cells to form, so stop being impatient. Worrying is a natural inhibitor of tumors, so stop worrying about things you can't control. Job 4:8 states, "According to what I have seen, those who plow iniquity and those who sow trouble harvest it." Remove yourself from the control of people who cause your discomfort, and when God reveals the core of your ailment, ask Him to release you from this bondage. If it's His will for that season that you might suffer, ask how can you endure the pain of this disease (discomfort)? Never divert from purpose, and never stop believing in what is true. Luke 9:62 says, "And Jesus said unto him, no man, having put his hand to the plow, and looking back, is fit for the kingdom of God." God has a purpose for us all, and it's not to suffer in vain for those who follow the truth. 2 Timothy 2:12 states, "If we suffer, we shall also reign with him: if we deny him, he also will deny us." If your purpose is to engage in spiritual combat, then war. If your purpose is to resist evil as an example before men, resist. If your purpose is to encourage, then encourage. If your purpose is to prophesy, then prophesy according to the revelations God has given you in its proper time and season. No matter what your purpose is, never lose hope. If God wants to use you to overcome cancer, then believe that you are an overcomer who may inherit the anointing to heal the sick.

My strongest charge unto those who believe is this: never give into the spirit of negativity. Negativity and irrational decisions will hinder you from fulfilling your purpose. When negativity presents itself before you, resist with the Word of truth and the power of purpose.

> *Casting down imaginations, and every high thing that exalteth itself against the knowledge of God, and bringing into captivity every thought to the obedience of Christ.*
> **-2 Corinthians 10:5**

Keep this in mind: I may be going through, but I will never lose faith. Jesus is Lord and Savior. Amen.

~ 18 ~

ONLY GOD CAN UNDERSTAND GOOD AND EVIL

Isaiah 45:7 speaks about the good, the bad, and their association with God. Each being is created for a specific purpose, and to deter from that purpose is sin. Sin violates God's commandments, which are His Holy Law and instructions. Any being who doesn't observe to do according to God's instructions, whether good or evil, will be found in error. Error is the result of sin, and the penalty for sin is death. Remember the evil spirit of the Lord sent to afflict King Saul? Romans 6:23 states, "For the wages of sin is death; but the gift of God is eternal life through Jesus Christ our Lord." The Lord has standards, and a part of those standards is balance and self-control, not self- ambition. Proverbs 25:28 states, "He that hath no rule over his own spirit is like a city that is broken down and without walls." Good and evil as it relates to the Most High is balance. Both forces exist within the principle of duality, providing sentient life forms (such as humans) with a choice.

The tree of wisdom (life) and the tree of the knowledge of good and evil are metaphysical constructs created by the Most High and planted within our minds. That's why we constantly battle with the enemy that is within to overcome the carnal self that the spirit man may rule over our members. If anyone doesn't function according to the purpose, they will be found in error unless they change their ways. 1 Corinthians 10:13 states, "There hath no temptation taken you but such as is common to man: but God is faithful, who will not suffer you to be tempted above that ye are able; but will with the temptation also make a way to escape, that ye may be able to bear it." How do we know that behavior can be controlled to a certain extent, if not entirely? The Word states that the spirit of a prophet is subject to a prophet, and Proverbs records the same as it relates to a king ruling over his spirit.

Regardless of the gift or call, one should never attempt to exalt themselves above the authority of the Most High. We can petition Him if confusion sets in our mind concerning suffering, such as the burden of the cross; however, He has the final say. We know that the Most High doesn't respond to the gift of the elected individual, but His response is towards the sincerity of the heart. Repentance helps us with self-reflection, forgiveness, and correction. Those who operate in wisdom understand her benefits, and the way of the wise is humility above all else. So, all are subject to the Most High, whether created to be good or evil. Nevertheless, God resists the proud but gives grace to the humble (James 4:6).

Brethren, let's pray:

Lord, I know what my nature is and the mandate that You have established in my life. Even though it sometimes brings me great pain, I don't desire to turn away from your righteous judgments and transgress your law. Please help me, Father, follow your way and desire the ancient paths of old, which is the way of righteousness according to your Word. I will be who you have called me to be, and nothing more or less. I know I'm here for a purpose so please help me define my purpose in you. And whatever you do, take not your Spirit away from me. Only you, Lord, can forgive and help me forgive myself and others without succumbing to fatal distractions. Glory be to Your name, now and forever. Amen!

CONCLUSION OF THE WHOLE MATTER

> *Let us hear the conclusion of the whole matter: Fear God, and keep his commandments: for this is the whole duty of man. For God shall bring every work into judgment, with every secret thing, whether it be good, or whether it be evil.*
> *-Ecclesiastes 12:13-14*

Choose wisdom, insight, and instructions over carnal thinking. The commandments of the Most High God are perfect, even to the conversion and conditioning of the soul. The Word says to be perfect even as your Father in Heaven is perfect (Matthew 5:48), and only the Word of truth can make you perfect. Christ states in John 14:15, "If you love me, keep my commandments." Those who love the Lord, their God, must observe His commandments and follow the instructions in the Spirit to attain heavenly wisdom, insight, sanctification, and salvation. The Most High and His Christ is the same yesterday, today, and forever.

Brethren, I pray your faith does not fail you in the way. Be blessed!

And hereby we do know that we know him, if we keep his commandments. He that saith, I know him, and keepeth not his commandments, is a liar, and the truth is not in him. But whoso keepeth his word, in him verily is the love of God perfected: hereby know we that we are in him. He that saith he abideth in him ought himself also so to walk, even as he walked.

-1 John 2:3-6

www.ingramcontent.com/pod-product-compliance
Lightning Source LLC
Chambersburg PA
CBHW022022290426
44109CB00015B/1277